Understanding Disabilities

UNDERSTANDING DEAFNESS

JESSICA RUSICK

Big Buddy Books
An Imprint of Abdo Publishing
abdobooks.com

abdobooks.com

Published by Abdo Publishing, a division of ABDO, PO Box 398166, Minneapolis, Minnesota 55439.

Printed in the United States of America, North Mankato, Minnesota
052021
092021

THIS BOOK CONTAINS RECYCLED MATERIALS

Design: Emily O'Malley, Mighty Media, Inc.
Production: Mighty Media, Inc.
Editor: Megan Borgert-Spaniol
Content Consultant: Brenda Blackmore, Special Education Director
Cover Photographs: Shutterstock Images
Interior Photographs: huePhotography/iStockphoto, p. 17 (bottom); 1001nights/iStockphoto, p. 17 (top); Shutterstock Images, pp. 4, 5, 7, 8, 9, 10, 11, 13, 15, 16, 18, 19, 20, 22, 23, 24, 25, 27, 28, 29; vgajic/ iStockphoto, p. 21

Library of Congress Control Number: 2020949912

Publisher's Cataloging-in-Publication Data
Names: Rusick, Jessica, author.
Title: Understanding deafness / by Jessica Rusick
Description: Minneapolis, Minnesota : Abdo Publishing, 2022 | Series: Understanding disabilities | Includes online resources and index.
Identifiers: ISBN 9781532195747 (lib. bdg.) | ISBN 9781098216474 (ebook)
Subjects: LCSH: Deafness--Juvenile literature. | Hearing disorders--Juvenile literature. | Deafness--Psychological aspects--Juvenile literature. | Social acceptance--Juvenile literature.
Classification: DDC 362.42--dc23

CONTENTS

Off to School

At 8:00 a.m., an alarm clock under Chloe's pillow **vibrates**. Chloe shuts it off and walks downstairs. She signs, "Good morning," to her parents and sits down for breakfast.

Chloe enjoys the quiet morning. After breakfast, she turns on her hearing aids. These will help her hear classmates at school.

Chloe is deaf. She **experiences** the world differently than hearing people. But she is like any other kid!

What Is Deafness?

Deafness is an inability to hear some or all sounds. Someone who is deaf has little to no hearing. People with milder hearing loss are sometimes called hard of hearing. However, many of these people also **identify** as deaf.

Deafness is an important part of a person's **identity**. Many deaf people have shared **experiences**. Because of this, some deaf people consider themselves part of a deaf community and **culture**.

Remember

People with disabilities are not **victims**. This word makes it sound like having a disability is a bad thing. But a disability is not bad. It's just a difference!

Common Behaviors in Deaf Culture

- Making strong eye contact
- Getting others' attention by lightly touching their arms or thumping a table
- Using sign language
- Standing farther apart when **communicating** to allow space for signing

It's important to accept and **appreciate** people's differences. Name-calling is never okay. And always respect how a deaf person chooses to **identify**. It's best to ask which kind of language a person prefers.

Hundreds of different sign languages exist across the world. The main one used in the United States is called American Sign Language, or ASL.

I am a person who is deaf.

Person First

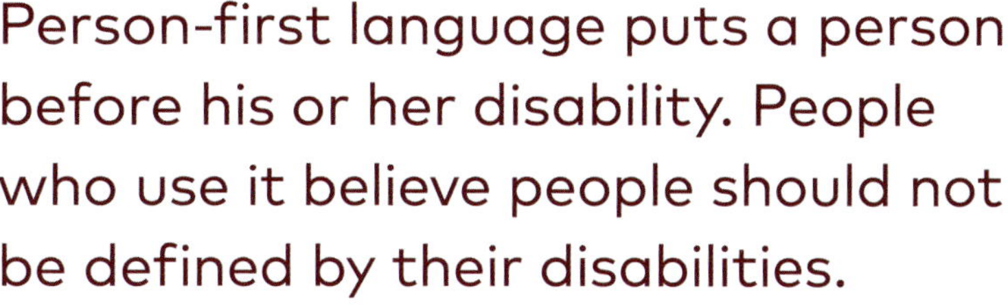

Person-first language puts a person before his or her disability. People who use it believe people should not be defined by their disabilities.

I am a deaf person.

Identity First

People who use **identity**-first language believe someone's disability is an important part of his or her identity. Some deaf people prefer to **identify** as such.

Who Is Deaf?

More than 400 million people in the world are deaf. Some people are deaf from the time they are born. Up to 3 out of every 1,000 children in the United States are born with hearing loss.

Other people become deaf because of illness or **injury**. A person can become deaf for these reasons at any age. In addition, it is common for people to **experience** hearing loss as they become older.

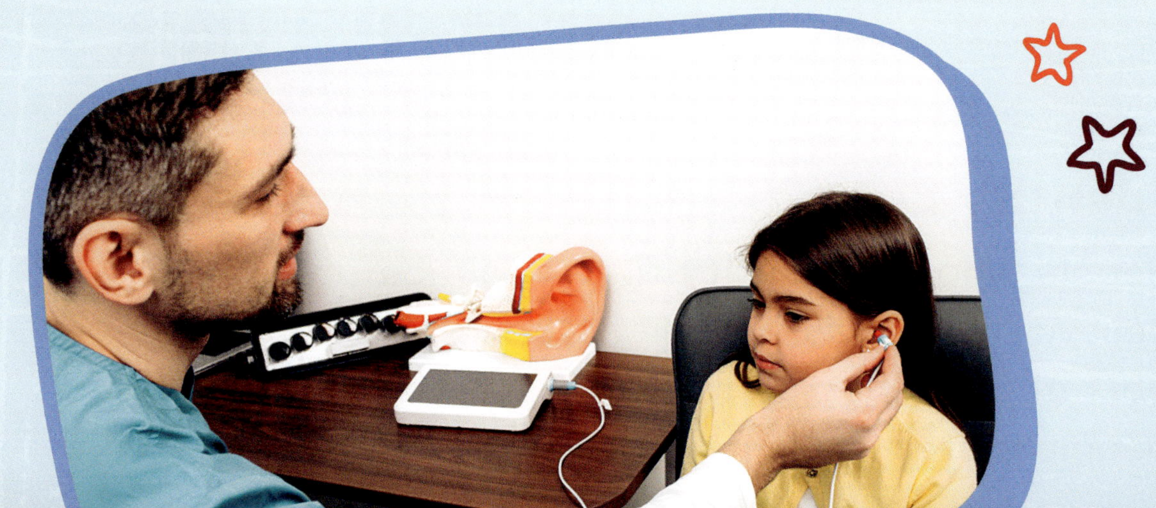

Doctors test the hearing of babies soon after birth.

Levels of Deafness

People **experience** different levels of deafness. These are mild, moderate, severe, and profound. Many deaf people can hear some sounds.

Someone with mild or moderate deafness can hear **conversation**. However, he or she may not hear everyone clearly. Someone with severe deafness may hear loud sounds, such as a passing truck. Someone with profound deafness may hear only very loud sounds or no sound at all.

Level of Deafness	Level of Sound that Can Be Heard	
Mild	Quiet **conversation**	
Moderate	Normal conversation with little background noise	
Severe	Heavy traffic, lawn mower	 
Profound	Jet engine, sirens, no sound	 

Hearing Devices

Some deaf kids wear hearing **devices**. One type of hearing device is a hearing aid. It makes sounds coming into the ear louder.

Another hearing device is a cochlear **implant**. This sends sounds directly to the brain as electrical currents. With a cochlear implant, voices can sound high-pitched and unnatural.

Some deaf people choose not to use hearing devices. They feel that by hearing, they are losing an important part of their deaf **identity**.

Hearing Aid

- Worn in or behind the ear
- Can help people with mild to moderate deafness understand speech
- Can help people with severe or profound deafness hear some sounds, but not understand speech

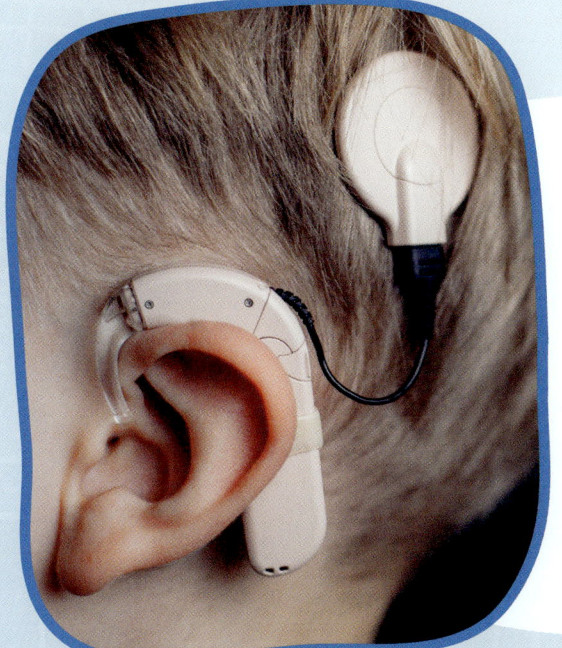

Cochlear Implant

- Worn behind the ear and under the skin
- Can help people with severe or profound deafness understand speech

Communication

Deaf kids **communicate** in several ways. They may use one, some, or all of the following methods:

Sign Language

Sign language is made up of hand and face movements. It allows people to communicate without using spoken words.

Spoken Language

Some deaf kids learn spoken language with the help of **speech therapists** and hearing **devices**.

Speech Reading

Speech reading means watching someone's face and mouth movements as he or she talks. Some deaf people use speech reading to understand what speaking people are saying.

Deafness at School

Some deaf children go to schools for deaf people. Here, classes are taught in sign language. Other deaf children learn in hearing classrooms. Different tools and practices help deaf children succeed in school.

A sign language interpreter can help a deaf child communicate with hearing individuals.

Teachers often use visual lessons for deaf kids.

Special devices turn spoken words into written words. This allows deaf kids to read what teachers and classmates say.

Social Challenges

Some deaf kids face social **challenges**. They may be unsure of how to **communicate** with hearing peers. Hearing kids also may not know how to start a **conversation** with a deaf person. So, deaf kids may feel lonely or left out.

Deaf kids may also be teased for appearing different. Hearing kids may not understand why a deaf person wears hearing **devices** or communicates differently. Being teased makes people feel bad about themselves.

Deaf people often play sports with hearing teammates. Team members decide together how to communicate during games.

Being a Friend

Everyone has his or her own strengths and **challenges**. That's okay! No matter what, everyone should be treated with respect.

Don't be afraid to start a **conversation** with a deaf classmate. Could you use your hands and face to **communicate**? Could you write messages to each other? Ask what your classmate prefers. Maybe you could learn a few sentences in sign language!

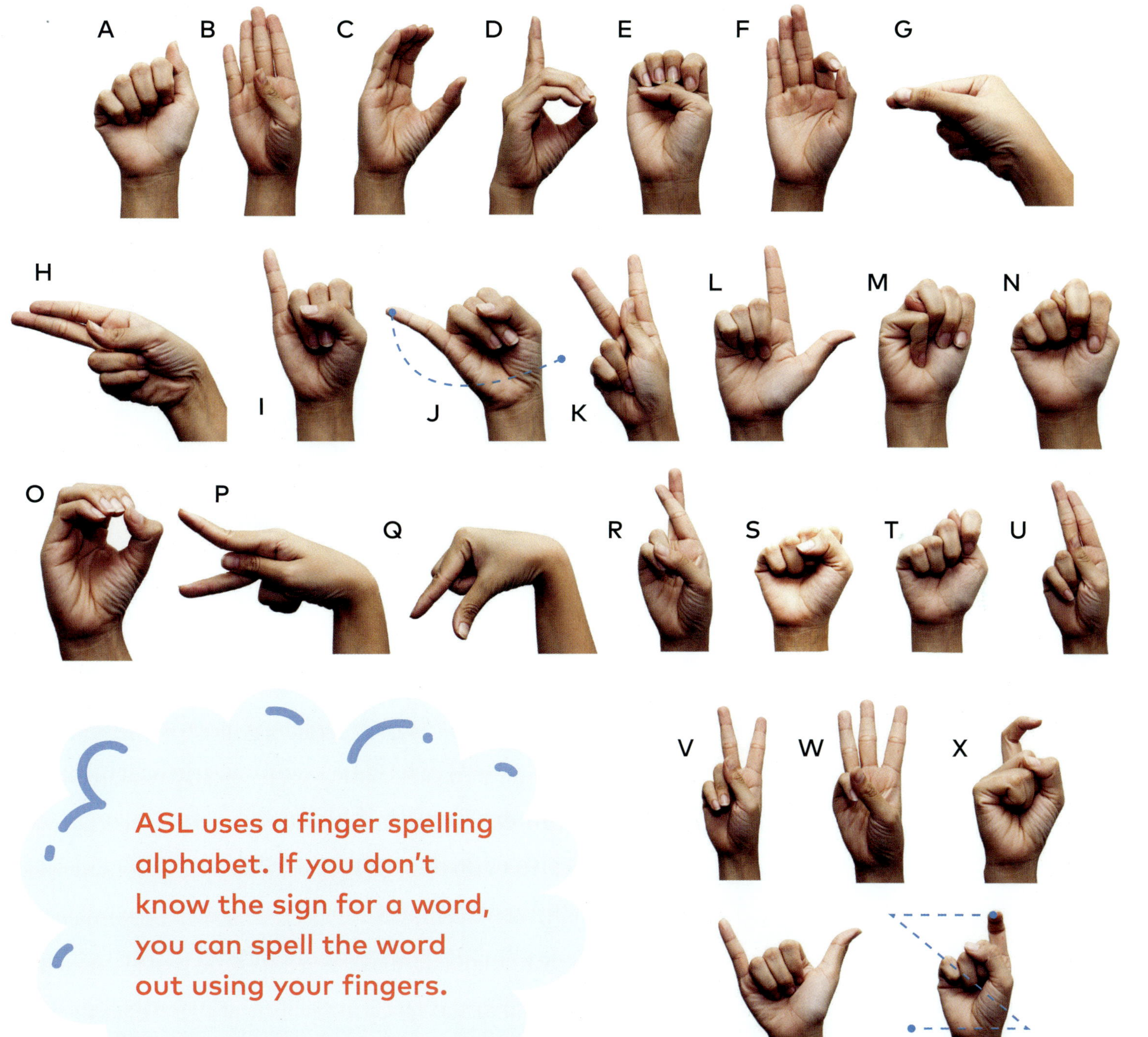

ASL uses a finger spelling alphabet. If you don't know the sign for a word, you can spell the word out using your fingers.

More Ways to Be a Friend

Speech Reading

If your friend speech reads, make sure he can see your mouth when you talk. Speak as you normally would.

Stand Up to Bullying

Tell an adult if your friend is being teased.

Speak to Your Friend

Speak directly to your friend and not your friend's **interpreter**. Your friend is the one you're **communicating** with!

Getting Attention

Politely wave or tap your friend's shoulder to get her attention.

Strengths

Being deaf can be **challenging**. However, many deaf people find their deafness makes them great listeners. This is because they must pay close attention when others are speaking. Deaf people have become successful actors, scientists, leaders, and more.

Millicent Simmonds

Millicent Simmonds is a deaf actress. She played deaf characters in the movies *Wonderstruck* and *A Quiet Place*. Simmonds hopes to encourage other people with disabilities to join the arts.

Millicent Simmonds wears a cochlear implant. But she mainly communicates using sign language.

Golden Rules

Millions of people have disabilities. If you know someone with a disability, there may be times when you feel unsure of what to say or do. When in doubt, remember to treat others how you'd want to be treated. And, keep in mind these other golden rules:

- Accept and respect differences
- Use respectful language
- Be kind and caring

Activities

Do you have a friend who is deaf? Invite him or her to join you for a fun activity.

Play a game or sport, such as freeze tag or tennis

Read a book together

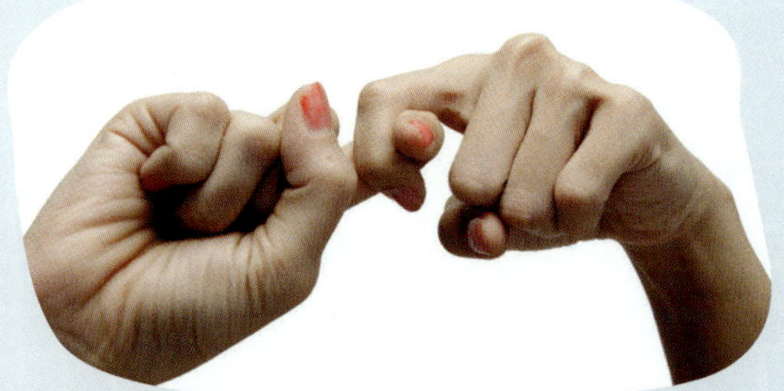

Ask to learn some words in sign language

GLOSSARY

appreciate—to value or admire greatly.

challenge (CHA-luhnj)—something that tests one's strengths or abilities.

communicate (kuh-MYOO-nuh-kayt)—to share knowledge, thoughts, or feelings.

conversation—a talk between two or more people.

culture (KUHL-chuhr)—the arts, beliefs, and ways of life of a group of people.

device—an object or machine that has a certain job.

experience—to do, see, feel, or be affected by something. Something that happens to you is an experience.

identify—to say or show who someone is.

identity—the set of features and beliefs that make a person who she or he is.

implant—a device put inside the body.

injury (IHN-juh-ree)—hurt or loss received.

interpreter—a person who turns the words of one language into those of another language.

speech therapist—a person who helps those with problems speaking learn how to say words correctly.

vibrate (VEYE-brayt)—to move back and forth very fast.

victim—someone who has been harmed by an unpleasant event.

ONLINE RESOURCES

To learn more about deafness, please visit **abdobooklinks.com** or scan this QR code. These links are routinely monitored and updated to provide the most current information available.

INDEX